FLIES

Oliver Lansley

FLIES

OBERON BOOKS
LONDON

WWW.OBERONBOOKS.COM

First published in 2011 by Oberon Books Ltd
Electronic edition published in 2012

Oberon Books Ltd
521 Caledonian Road, London N7 9RH
Tel: +44 (0) 20 7607 3637 / Fax: +44 (0) 20 7607 3629
e-mail: info@oberonbooks.com
www.oberonbooks.com

A catalogue record for this book is available from the British
Library.

PB ISBN: 978-1-84943-214-6
Digital ISBN: 978-1-84943-592-5

Cover design by Zoe Squire

Contents

4

Foreword

BY DIRECTOR EMMA EARLE

Flies is an absurdist tale of one man's struggle to overcome his acute irrational fear and the way that fear manifests itself, takes hold and governs.

After an unfortunate incident on a flight, Dennis must undergo six weeks of therapy to address his issues. Fragments of the memories and experiences that have shaped his fear provide the backbone of the play as we yo-yo back and forth in time, from school trips to a petting zoo, to working as a dental assistant. But will Dennis conquer his fear before The Fly – a charming, whisky drinking maverick with a thoroughly nasty streak – takes up permanent residence in his consciousness? Or will he cave in and let the fear beat him? Dennis' obsessive-compulsive behaviour as he endeavours to create a world without flies is both comical and tragic; indeed we feel as though we are literally in a front-row seat inside his brain, witnessing his nightmares and accompanying him in his flights of fantasy.

We meet a variety of characters from his life – ex-girlfriends, ex-employers, ex-teachers…you get the picture. And throughout the play we are invited to question the reliability of the witness. Voices, faces and places take on a warped, kaleidoscopic quality – all of them projections from Dennis' consciousness, some more malevolent than others.

This is Pins and Needles' second major collaboration with Oliver Lansley following *Ernest and the Pale Moon*. With an exciting live soundtrack from experimental, Bristol-based musician Kid Carpet, our production is a fusion of theatre, stand-up comedy and a gig.

Oliver's play ends with a startling metamorphosis: Dennis' ultimate act of defiance and release, in which the real world collides with the surreal.

Introduction

BY OLIVER LANSLEY

Flies was an interesting proposition for me. The director Emma, with whom I've collaborated many times, came to me with a title 'Flies', a character name, Dennis, and dates for a proposed run of this show that didn't even exist yet!

It's an interesting way to start on a project but Emma knows I am always intrigued by a challenge and when she said she wanted to create something that was a cross between *Metamorphosis* and *Jaws* I was hooked!

It's hard to say much about the piece itself as I don't think it's the sort of play that benefits from the reader being given too much information. It's a play to be explored rather than explained.

What I did know was that I wanted to replicate the fractured, disjointed workings of Dennis' brain in telling his story. Creating literally a 'web' of information that all somehow spirals around a centre point (the fly in the middle of that web).

It jumps around in time and space and reality and is in many senses a stream of consciousness. This was very much reflected in the way that I wanted to write it. Allowing information to pour out randomly, some obviously relevant, some more obscure, like fragments torn out at random from a well-worn diary.

As for the fly, the very first words that I wrote for the whole play were – *'I took a shit on your food'* – this seemed to set out quite a clear path to me as to who this character was!

What is real, what is not and how do we know the difference? *Flies* is an odd little play, but then Dennis is an odd little man...

THE BREWERY
TOBACCO FACTORY THEATRE

Flies by Oliver Lansley was first performed on 4th October 2011 at the Tobacco Factory's Brewery Theatre, Bristol.

Produced by Pins and Needles Productions.

Original cast:

DENNIS, Oliver Hollis

THE FLY and other roles, Paul Mundell

Live music performed by Kid Carpet

Written by Oliver Lansley
Director, Emma Earle
Design, Zoe Squire
Lighting Design, Anna Barrett
Composer, Kid Carpet
Animator, Becca Rose
Costume Supervisor, Bianca Ward
Assistant Producer, Lee Rayner
Stage Manager, Katie Barrett

Artwork created by Zoe Squire

Pins and Needles Productions is committed to creating inspiring visual theatre that unites both physical and text based work. We are interested in telling highly theatrical stories for young and old, and enjoy making work that encourages the audience to take an imaginative leap. The company was established in 2009 by Director/Designer partnership Emma Earle and Zoe Squire. www.pinsandneedlesproductions.co.uk

This production was supported by the National Lottery through Arts Council England. *Flies* was inspired by an original concept by Toby Farrow and developed in association with Bristol Ferment at Bristol Old Vic.

With special thanks to the Earles, the Squires and everyone else who helped to make this production happen.

LOTTERY FUNDED

We open in a Winter Wonderland. A fantastical dream version of Antarctica. Snow, polar bears etc. Happy music plays.

Suddenly we move from this to find DENNIS, sitting cramped and uncomfortable in a plane seat. He stares at the ice in his plastic glass, the fantasy shattered.

He looks agitated.

Next to him is an obese woman wearing thick glasses.

We hear DENNIS' thoughts.

DENNIS: *(V.O.)* I listen to the gentle *chink chink* of the ice rattling around in my plastic cup, which I grip tightly in my right hand.

Chink chink chink.

My hand is shaking, rattling the cup, making the ice chink.

Chink chink chink.

I'm not a good flyer. Something about being cooped up in a confined space, a lack of control, a…

SNAP!

The flimsy plastic of my cup cracks in my hand, gripped too tight. Ice cold water, melted from the chinking ice, runs into my lap.

WOMAN: Oopsy daisy.

DENNIS: *(V.O.)* Says the obese lady next to me, flowery
dress, the kind of thick glasses I didn't even know
existed any more.
She grins at me, her rubbery jowls expanding like
a pink balloon.
I attempt to smile back…
But know that my face is contorted into some kind
of strange grimace, like a constipated baby or a
bowl of chicken soup whose croutons have floated
into the form of an expression – like when Jesus
appears in toast. Although Jesus doesn't appear in
toast because Jesus doesn't exist or if he does he
doesn't appear in toast.
She spots the mania in my eyes and is visibly
perturbed.
I feel bad for a moment but take solace in the fact
that she may not speak to me again.
She does.

WOMAN: Not a good Flyer?

DENNIS: *(V.O.)* I'm not a good flyer.

WOMAN: Just relax it'll be over before you know it.

DENNIS: *(V.O.)* I feel the ropes inside my stomach twist
around my organs, wringing them out like damp
cloths. It takes everything in my control not to
punch her in her stupid fat face.
Not because I don't like her, not because she's
done anything wrong, she's been very nice. It's just
a physical reaction, a powerful urge. An attempt to
smash the fear bundled inside me. Smash it in its
stupid fat face.

I grip the cup tighter in my hand, crushing the plastic further, and feel the cool water run down my leg.
I attempt another smile and nod.
She nods back, then opens her magazine.
I console myself in the thought that very soon my life will change forever. I will be free.

DENNIS addresses the audience.

DENNIS: My life does change.
But sadly not in the way I was hoping for.

–

FLY appears. He wears an immaculately crisp suit. He holds a glass of whisky and gently 'chinks' the ice. He is cool, calm and collected and takes his time with his delivery. He is very charming.

FLY: I took a shit on your food…
I know it's what we 'do' – I know it's an action I am genetically predisposed to undertake – but I just wanted you to know that this was different.
I wanted you to know that on this occasion, this specific act of defecation was for one reason and one reason only and that is that… I don't like you. There.
I took a shit on your food and then I vomited and then I stamped around in it with my little sticky feet and it was all because I don't like you.
I don't like your stupid face.
I don't like your stupid life.
I don't like anything about you.

He takes a big sigh as if relieved of a burden.

Ahhh, I'm glad I got that off my chest – feels good to clear the air doesn't it?

–

A young boy, GEORGE MACMILLAN, *appears.*

DENNIS: One of my first memories is of a boy at school pulling the wings off one. His name was...

GEORGE: George Macmillan.

DENNIS: ...the boy.

He had caught it somehow – It was one of those big, horrible, fat ones, it had been banging relentlessly at the window for hours and had become dozy, disorientated. He coaxed it onto a piece of card and then pushed a pin through its abdomen.

I watch its poor legs curl in with pain. But it didn't die, they kept moving, feeling around as if trying to pull the pin out. But it had no real fight to it.

George with his fat little fingers reached down and grabbed one of the wings and, as if he were picking a grape from a tree, he just...

GEORGE: ...plucked it right off.

DENNIS: Another weak flex of the legs.

There was no discernible pleasure or excitement on George's face. Not even any curiosity, just a strange passive inevitability. Like he was doing what had to be done.

He delicately placed the wing down then reached in and plucked the second one. This one was not

so clean, it tore in the process and only just over half came away.
I remember him holding it up.

GEORGE: To see if he could see through it.

DENNIS: The creature's legs continued to move for a while.
George watched it, and I watched it.
Then he pulled out the pin, held the card up to the window and with a puff of air blew the fly away.
It was over.

–

A DOCTOR lounges by his desk, talking into a Dictaphone.

DOCTOR: After the…incident, the patient has been referred to me for examination and assessment. I am to determine whether or not this man poses a threat…

He stops the tape, rewinds it and plays it back.

(DOCTOR on dictaphone.) …Poses a threat…poses a threat… poses a threat…

DOCTOR: Note to self, I do not like the way my voice sounds on an audio tape – a.) Investigate whether this is the way my voice sounds to other people, b.) Get Janet to look into other forms of audio recording…

He starts recording again.

...On initial examination it appears the patient is suffering from acute Pteronarcophobia: an almost devastating fear of flies.

Possibly stemming from an unfavourable incident in his childhood, something involving his father or an uncle or a monster under the bed, or a clown, perhaps a clown dressed as a fly who crept into his bed and touched him or argued with his mother as he played in the next room pretending not to listen. These are just speculations of course, I have no idea if any of the above suggestions actually took place. However in my professional opinion I believe they did. Some, if not all, of the above... Note to self. Probe deeper re. clowns, parents, paedos... Peadofly!

He pulls out a note book and writes down 'Paedofly'.

–

DENNIS: I have a routine. To help me.
I put sellotape over all the cracks and the holes. The plug sockets, the keyholes.
I have draught excluders on every door. They look like long sausage dogs. They are made from a colourful carpet material and they have faces which makes them friendly as well as useful, allowing me to look at them without constantly being reminded of their purpose.
I have given them all names.
Desmond, Rupert, Basil, Shirley, Dozy, Droopy and Pete Reynolds.

The toilets are covered with clingfilm when not in use and the plugs must always be kept in the plugholes.
I don't have a bin inside. All my rubbish goes directly outside, but when I'm disposing of it I have to wear the mask.
It's like a beekeeper's mask; I bought it from an online auction site. It belonged to a man from the West Country, who may or may not have kept bees.
Windows are painted shut.

...It is sometimes awkward to explain when I have guests...

If I have guests.

But everyone has their little rituals right?
We all have our own little foibles?

–

DOCTOR: I have recommended the subject return for an undefined number of sessions so that we may figuratively wrestle with the problem. How long this shall take is hard to say. I would like a new couch for my office, and once I have a new couch I may need a new lamp to match. I shall assess the case on a rolling basis.
...Note to self. Perhaps a plastic sheet for the new couch, like what you put on mattresses for children who can't stop wetting the bed. It's the tears, they're what caused the rot... must be the salt. Bloody babies.

He seems an affable chap if a tad...troubled. In our session he spoke at length about an incident involving a school trip to a local farm, where he became separated from his class –

DENNIS: I was nine and we were visiting Goldsworth Farm and Petting Zoo. We had taken the forms, got them signed by our mums, brought in the seven pounds in an envelope and now, thanks to a school minibus which smelled of cheese puffs and future disappointment, we were finally there.

I was particularly looking forward to petting a giant tortoise, like the ones from those islands that David Attenborough likes.

I had a book about zoos, which I loved to read. Full of lions and tigers and killer whales and penguins.

Goldsworth Petting Zoo was not like this.

Sheep, pigs, dogs, rabbits, cows, guinea pigs and a lama...

Class 4b were not impressed.

They did however have three normal sized tortoises.

And it was the tortoises that led to...the incident.

I wanted to pick one up, I wanted to feel what its belly was like, if it was soft like dough rising in a bowl or hard, like a wooden egg.

As my class were led away to watch Agatha, a giant brown and white splotched cow, be milked, I hung back.

The tortoises were in with the rabbits and guinea pigs, just wandering around munching the grass nonchalantly, sometimes popping their head in and out of their shells. Sometimes just sitting there. I spotted one by the fence, next to a large open wooden box.

If I reached the full length of my arm over the fence the tips of my middle fingers could just brush the top of its shell. It was hard and quite cool. I put my feet in the wire holes of the fence and clambered up as high as I could, stretching out my arm. Unbeknown to the poor tortoise my fingers crept along its back, tiptoeing towards its stomach. Just as they reached the lip of its shell, my foot slipped and I jerked backwards, flipping the unsuspecting tortoise onto its back.

I watched it through the wire fence doing, what I assume is the tortal version of being terrified. This consists of slowly moving your arms and legs around, and occasionally bobbing your head back and forth.

I panicked. I immediately recalled a story my friend had told me about how if a tortoise got stuck upside down it would cook in the sun like a Cornish pasty. I leapt to my feet and started climbing the fence again, this time with reckless abandon, determined to right the poor tortoise and save him from his fate. But as I reached out, stretching as far as my puny nine-year-old arms would take me, I lost my balance and tumbled down over the fence, almost somersaulting into a large wooden box. I lay there for a moment. The puff knocked out of me. There was a smell, an awful smell. And that's when I heard it…

The buzzing…

We are suddenly back with the DOCTOR again.

DOCTOR: …He fell into a pile of compost, decomposing fruit, vegetables and the like. Food for the animals. He mentioned something about…

He presses play on his Dictaphone.

(DENNIS on dictaphone.) Flies rising like a cloud of dust from a beaten carpet.

DOCTOR: …and seeing…

(DENNIS on dictaphone.) Maggots!

DOCTOR: Crawling from the translucent brown skins of the decomposing apples that his fingers pierced as he scrambled around trying to get to his feet…
All very dramatic, though I suspect totally irrelevant.
MMM… I shall pursue *Paedofly* with vigour.

–

DENNIS: It is the presence of a single pair of wings that distinguishes true f…flies from other insects with the word in their name. May…f…lies, Dragon…f…lies, Damsel…f…lies, Snake…f…lies, Saw…f…lies, Caddis…f…lies, butter…f…lies… These are *not…f…*
The *True* ones are insects of the order Diptera which means 'two wings'. Most insects have four wings. However in their case, over time, this second set of wings has developed into small, stumpy knobs which are located behind the main wings. These help keep them steady and balanced,

making them very…agile and able to manoeuvre themselves into intricate flight patterns, they can hover, they can spin, they can even go backwards.

FLY: You remember the old woman who swallowed a fly? That was me.
I don't know why, but she did it. And then she went through this whole palaver, swallowing a spider, that wriggled and wiggled and jiggled inside her, then she had to swallow a bird to catch the spider, which was pretty absurd. Then a cat to catch the bird, a dog to catch the cat, a goat to catch the dog, which of course is ludicrous but I guess by this point she just wasn't thinking straight. Soon followed a cow and so on and so forth, until she finally ended up swallowing a horse. A whole horse. In one go… alive!? Can you even imagine that? How she managed to get that thing down her neck, a live horse! – An awful affair, she died of course.

DENNIS: A house…fly maggot can hatch within 24 hours if the place where the eggs are laid is warm and moist.

FLY: *The Fly*? Remember *The Fly*? That poor scientist who'd spent all that time doing that experiment, the teleportation thing, with the pods and what not. And he finally figured it out, how to make it work and he built up the courage to test it but then when he did this little fly flew into the pod with him. And so the poor guy ended up having his genes spliced and then he became this hideous half-man, half-fly creature, and his ears fell off, and his teeth fell out and his fingernails came off.

...Awful business.

He died of course.

But that fly? That was me.

DENNIS: During the Spanish-American War in 1898, they spread typhoid and killed over 5,000 soldiers. The battles in the war itself only killed 4,000 soldiers...

...Making them worse than war.

FLY: Do you remember when you saw that programme? With all the poor starving African babies, who were dying? They had no food, no water, nothing, and these flies would just, constantly be buzzing around their faces. Buzz buzz buzz.

You remember that one poor creature, crying for their mother, not knowing why this was happening to them.

You remember watching it on your telebox, how helpless you felt. Angry, powerless, pathetic, greedy, selfish, ungrateful.

Sitting there eating your cakes, and drinking your pop.

You remember watching as a fly landed on the poor creature's face and they didn't even have the energy to swat him away, to move their hand, and the fly crawled over their face, over their little cheeks and into their mouth.

That was me.

Sorry but it was, guilty as charged.

DENNIS: I have what I'm told is an 'irrational' fear.

Stupid. What is a *rational* fear?

Sharks…bears? How many sharks and bears have
you ever seen?
My fear is 'irrational' because it 'poses no real
threat'…
5,000 men! Soldiers! That's an army…no real
threat?!

FLY: Exodus 8:20-32 – This is what the LORD says:
Let my people go, so that they may worship
me. If you do not let my people go, I will send
swarms of flies upon you and your officials, on
your people and into your houses… The houses
of the Egyptians will be full of flies, and even the
ground…

DENNIS: The sound the…that thin, high…zzzzzzzzz.
Like a needle, like a dentist's implement drilling
into the back of my head.
The way they move the jerky, patternless…there's
no sense to it, no path; it's anarchy, chaos.
Their black, thick, wiry limbs, their little feet tap-
tap-tapping.
Their mouths, their teeth, dripping, lustful, disease-
carrying, dirty, filthy…
Their eyes, hundreds and thousands of eyes,
staring.

FLY: …That's me, all me, every single one of them.

DENNIS: I feel them, carrying this stench, this decay,
bringing it all to me.

FLY: In 1955 Emily Dickenson wrote a poem…

DENNIS: An army, rising up, like plumes of smoke
from a volcano, living ash wanting to settle on me
and bury me and suffocate me.
All of them. Looking for me. Wanting me to fail.
They know, they want to find me. It's me or them.
They are many, they are legion.

FLY: I heard a fly buzz when I died;
The stillness round my form
Was like the stillness in the air
Between the heaves of storm.

The eyes beside had wrung them dry,
And breaths were gathering sure
For that last onset, when the king
Be witnessed in his power.

I willed my keepsakes, signed away
What portion of me I
Could make assignable, – and then
There interposed a fly,

With blue, uncertain, stumbling buzz,
Between the light and me;
And then the windows failed, and then
I could not see to see.

– That fly she heard...

Me.

I don't know why.

–

DENNIS is back in his plane seat.

DENNIS: The flight was from what I remember actually fairly smooth.

DENNIS: *(V.O.)* Every now and then a rumble of turbulence gives the cabin a teasing shake, causing me to grip my arm rests and chew the inside of my cheeks.

And every time this happens the fat face turns to me, smug and patronising, like she was looking at a monkey who'd attended a firework display and didn't like the bangs.

WOMAN: Bumpedy bump.

DENNIS: *(V.O.)* I find it hard to disguise my contempt. A tray of inedible space food is offered. Potatoes and meat, sloshed together in a plastic tray. Boxes of it, all piling up, discarded, dirty, open, an invitation to…
I politely decline.

WOMAN: I am so hungry… I could eat a horse.

DENNIS: *(V.O.)* I turn and look out of the window next to me.
Clouds, sky, sun.
I lean back against my chair and the sweat on my back starts soaking into my shirt.
I close my eyes.
And that's when I hear it…

–

DENNIS: I don't know when the tipping point was.
The point where things shifted from inconvenient

to untenable. The day that I locked the door
and didn't open it again. The day I painted my
windows shut.
I look for it, trying to find the moment, the
moment where I just...gave up.
Gave in and let them beat me.

*A DENTIST walks in. As he speaks we see him carrying out a
procedure on an unsuspecting patient. His assistant hands him
various implements.*

DENTIST: I'm sorry Dennis but I'm going to have to let
you go.

DENNIS: Was it was when I lost my job?

DENTIST: I'm afraid your behaviour yesterday resulted
in a number of complaints.

DENNIS: I was a Dental Assistant. As long as I could
remember I always wanted to be a Dental
Assistant. Not a Dentist.

DENTIST: Mrs Wilshire was particularly terrified when
you locked yourself in the X-ray room with her.

DENNIS: *(To DENTIST.)* I didn't even know she was in
there!

(To us.)

I wanted to be the one who holds the suction hose,
who hands over the correct instruments, who gives
you the goggles, and a cup of water and tells you to
rinse.

DENTIST: Nevertheless she said your behaviour was most disturbing. The shaking, crying…

DENNIS: I loved that job. I felt at home in the Dentist's surgery, everything was so white and clean.

DENTIST: We simply can't risk something like that happening again.

DENNIS: I was happy…

(To DENTIST.)

Please, I can explain.

DENTIST: I'm sorry…

The DENTIST begins to address the audience directly. Meanwhile his ASSISTANT carries on with the patient in the background. However the procedure gets more ludicrous and soon he starts forcing cats, dogs, goats etc. down her throat – like the old woman who swallowed a fly.

Dennis was assisting me with a particularly tricky canine root filling. It was a hot day and I had opened the window to let in some air.
As I asked Dennis to pass me a periodontal probe I looked over to find him frozen, like a statue, ears pricked up like a hunting dog, listening – A terrible fear in his eyes.

DENNIS: I had heard it, the buzzing.

DENTIST: Before I knew it he was screaming. He jumped to his feet, knocking my instruments all over the place, before running out of the door, down the hall and locking himself in the X-ray room.

DENNIS: It caught me off guard; I didn't even know the bloody window was open!

DENTIST: We have a special room for X-rays: it's lined with lead, to protect us from the radiation.

DENNIS: It seemed like the sensible place to go at the time.

DENTIST: Unfortunately Mrs Wilshire was in the middle of having her teeth X-rayed and she did not take kindly to a strange man running in screaming, locking the door and immediately collapsing into a foetal wreck.

DENNIS: It was perhaps a slight overreaction but it had landed on my hand for God's sake, it touched me! I just…lost it.

DENTIST: She was not happy.

DENNIS: I didn't even notice she was in there until I opened my eyes and saw her feet dangling over the edge of the chair.

DENTIST: *(To DENNIS.)* I'm sorry Dennis…I think you should think about getting some help.

DENNIS: *(To AUDIENCE.)* It could have been then…or when my girlfriend left me?

DENNIS looks expectantly at the DENTIST, who is unsure what to do, he takes off his 'dentist' costume and adopts 'girlfriend stance'

GIRLFRIEND: Technically, I wasn't his girlfriend...we'd met two, maybe three times...

DENNIS: She's being shy but really she was my girlfriend. We kissed.

GIRLFRIEND: I was drunk.

DENNIS: She stayed over at my house, in my bed.

GIRLFRIEND: But I don't think we ever said, I'll be your girlfriend, you be my boyfriend.

DENNIS: Well no but, do people ever say that?

GIRLFRIEND: I've said it before.

DENNIS: Fine, well what would you call it?

GIRLFRIEND: Look it's not a big deal. Just...carry on.

DENNIS: I think my obsession, my fear, must have gotten too much for her.

GIRLFRIEND: ...To be honest I wasn't even aware of...

DENNIS: I didn't like going out to parks or restaurants. I had all these weird rituals and I think it just drove her away. She didn't like seeing me suffer like this.

GIRLFRIEND: I was actually seeing another guy at the time, I met him through work. Steven, he was really nice.

DENNIS: Yep, it just drove her away.

GIRLFRIEND: Right, as I say, technically that's not what...

DENNIS: Drove her right away – This damn phobia.

GIRLFRIEND: Are you listening to me?

DENNIS: It's ruined my life.

GIRLFRIEND: Fine.

GIRLFRIEND leaves. DENNIS revels in the fantasy of his relationship for a moment before his heart sinks.

DENNIS: One day I just woke up, and I realised I had barely left my house in a month. My home was no longer my home but a fortress. Nothing got in, nothing got out. I was re-breathing my own breath. In my head everything that was wrong with my life came down to this one thing, to these...things, these creatures, their decay and stink, spreading through my entire life until there was nothing left. They had contaminated it, they were holding me prisoner.
I knew something had to change. That I had to get out.

–

DOCTOR: Progress with the patient has been slow, in fact, I'm not sure it's progress at all, the opposite in fact... I must say he is a bleak fellow, depresses me a bit spending time with him if I'm honest, he's a real downer, always complaining or moaning about something... The man has issues.
Considering wrapping up the treatment early if he doesn't cheer up soon though am still a considerable number of sessions away from couch.

...Saw a wonderful Edwardian Chesterfield, but shipping alone was into the hundreds...

Have told the patient that he must attempt to confront the fear, tackle it head on, give it a face and smash the face into oblivion. No good blubbering and squealing, all curled up.

He's such a baby.

He must fight...rise up and defeat it, he must –

Oooh yes before I forget 590 seconds on Minesweeper today – on expert – note to self get Janet to check Minesweeper world records and submit, must be in with a shot.

–

We hear a typing sound.

DENNIS: F...L...Y – Search!

876,000,000 results... Hmmm, new page.

N...O... F...L...Y – Search!

101,000,000 results – Better...ok so what do we have here... Aha! List of 'no-fly' zones! Perfect! What have we got...Libya... Israel... Pakist-

Hang on... Oh... no that's not...right...of course...

New page

F...L...Y...D...O...N...T...L...I...V...E... –

search

622,000,000, no

F...L...Y...N...O...T...H...E...R...E...

131,000,000, No

W...H...E...R...E...N...O...F...L...I...E...S...? –

SEARCH

17,300,000 results.

No, no, nope, no...

Stop…click…there…that's it.

–

DENNIS enters a TRAVEL AGENTS.

TRAVEL AGENT: Hello there sir what can I do for you today?

DENNIS: Hi, er, I'd like to book a ticket to Antarctica?

The TRAVEL AGENT taps on her keyboard.

TRAVEL AGENT: Ant…arctic…a. Right sir and is the trip business or pleasure?

DENNIS: Er neither…pleasure? More pleasure than…

She types again.

TRAVEL AGENT: Pleeea…suuure… Ok and are you looking for flights *and* accommodation?

DENNIS: Yep, yes I will need somewhere to sta…

She types again.

TRAVEL AGENT: Staaaaay… – and how long are you looking to stay for?

DENNIS: Forever.

She stops, stares at him, then types slowly.

TRAVEL AGENT: For…ev…er.

There is a long awkward pause.

DENNIS: I have an illness…and, I've heard it will be better over there.

TRAVEL AGENT: *I see.*

DENNIS: It's…there's something that doesn't agree with me, that I don't like and I've heard they don't have that thing in Antarctica, so, that would be good for me… I mean, I say I don't like it but I'm being… I'm probably underselling it, it's bad… I can't… I find it hard to… I have to cover my toilet in clingfilm.

She continues to stare at him.

TRAVEL AGENT: …Because of the illness?

DENNIS: Right… I mean, technically it's not really an illness, it's a phobia – a fear, it's supposedly an 'irrational' fear but… What's rational right!? Are we…rational? You know rational is a…it's a, it's subjective right, if…what are you afraid of?

TRAVEL AGENT: Cancer?

DENNIS: Cancer right, well that's…you know you could say that's irrational, it's not like cancer's gonna, it's not like cancer can just come and find you, come and get you, cancer can't hide under your bed! There's no real reason why you should be scared of cancer…you know? Why you're any more likely to get it…so it's, you know, in a way it's…you're irrational too, why are *you* scared of cancer more than me? Why are you any more likely to get cancer than I am?

TRAVEL AGENT: My mother died of cancer.

DENNIS: *(Stumbling.)* Wow she…? Really? She? Ok so
then, yes I guess that makes…so yes, you have a
reason to… Well that's fine then, I can see there is a
certain rationale… behind…
Ok so wouldn't you…if you could, if you knew
that cancer couldn't survive in Antarctica then
wouldn't you move there?

TRAVEL AGENT: Can it?

DENNIS: What?

TRAVEL AGENT: Can it survive there?

DENNIS: *(Getting frustrated.)* Cancer? I don't know.
I'm being hypothe… I mean maybe it can't? It is
colder and that makes it harder for things to…
Look it doesn't really… My point is that *if* it
couldn't, and *if* you could move there to get away
from cancer then wouldn't you do it?

She thinks about this.

TRAVEL AGENT: I don't know…don't they have polar
bears there?

DENNIS: You're scared of polar bears?

TRAVEL AGENT: Isn't everyone scared of polar bears?

DENNIS: There you see there! That! Now that *is*
an irrational fear, we're in Leicester. There is
absolutely no way that a polar bear is going to…
Polar bears pose no threat to you…

TRAVEL AGENT: No threat? Are you crazy a polar bear could rip your arms off!

DENNIS: Right but it's not...that's not going to happen.

TRAVEL AGENT: How do you know?!

DENNIS: Because we're in LEICESTER!

TRAVEL AGENT: One could escape?

DENNIS: Look there's no polar bears ok, polar bears live at the North Pole, Antarctica is the South Pole, it is as far as you can possibly be from polar bears ok, there are no polar bears...

She looks at him unconvinced.

DENNIS: So would you move there?

TRAVEL AGENT: Would my friends be there?

DENNIS: ...no

TRAVEL AGENT: How about my family, would they be coming with me?

DENNIS: ...no, but –

TRAVEL AGENT: Would I even have a job or anything?

DENNIS: Well I guess you'll try and find one while you're out there.

TRAVEL AGENT: ...I've got to say it doesn't sound great.

Beat.

TRAVEL AGENT: I think I'll probably stick it out here.

DENNIS: But what about the cancer?

TRAVEL AGENT: I think I'd rather the cancer had something that was worth taking.

DENNIS just looks at her.

DENNIS: I've just sold everything I own.

Beat.

TRAVEL AGENT: Oh…

Beat.

TRAVEL AGENT: Do they have wolves there?

DENNIS doesn't want to talk about this anymore.

DENNIS: No.

TRAVEL AGENT: Not even like arctic wolves?

DENNIS: No because it's the *Antarctic, ANT*-arctic. There are definitely no wolves there.

TRAVEL AGENT: Are wolves the thing that you're scared of?

He snaps.

DENNIS: Can I just buy a plane ticket please?

TRAVEL AGENT starts typing.

–

DENNIS: Since I was about ten years old I have, at least once a month without fail, had the same dream.

I am at Westcliff swimming baths. I'm wearing nothing but a tiny pair of illuminous green swimming trunks and a pair of goggles. I'm standing at the deep end looking in. Far at the other end of the pool is my old swimming teacher, Mr Graham, who claps his hands impatiently, telling me to jump. I don't want to because it's deep and the water's cold but he just stares at me and claps his hands aggressively. His face crumpled into a frown. His beaked nose and wild white eyebrows darting off in all directions giving his gaunt face a strange avian quality.

He claps his hands, I pull the goggles over my eyes and I fall forward, head first into the water.

I close my eyes tightly as I submerge and suddenly I am aware of a strange unpleasant sensation, scratching, creeping all over my body. And this noise, this horrible noise. Which starts almost like crumpling paper. I open my eyes but instead of cool, clear blue water everything is black. As my eyes adjust I see that it is moving. The blackness is swirling and swarming all around me. I begin to realise that rather than swimming in water I am in a deep thick swarm of fat, buzzing f…lies.

I start to panic and lash around, trying to make my way to the surface. As I do my breathing gets heavy and I gulp for breath, I start to swallow the flies, feeling them buzzing down my throat. The noise is deafening, the buzzing, like electricity running through my brain. Like a thousand tiny screams. I gasp around, my arms and legs flailing, feeling the tiny wings cracking and crunching underneath. Thousands of black wiry legs, pinching and sticking to my skin.

I don't know what's up or down, but I feel like I'm sinking, or falling.

I scream.

Then suddenly I feel something grab my arm, a tight grip. With great strength it wrenches my ten-year-old body up and out, plonking me down on the poolside.

My body is red, and scratched, I'm shaking, I catch my breath, pull off my goggles, and wipe the tears from my eyes. I look up at the person who saved me.

And standing there in front of me is this huge, fat, black f...

He stands on two legs and is giant, much taller than me, the size of a fully grown man but much thicker and wider. I stare at him and he looks down at me. Those strange alien eyes observing me, emotionless.

We stand there for what feels like a long time, staring at one another. I notice its wings seem damaged, like they have been patched up and stuck back on somehow – they're a mess.

After a while he slowly reaches out and takes my shoulders, pulling me towards him.

Then, suddenly, he opens his mouth and out of it pours this stuff, it shoots forwards towards me, a flood, and just as I feel it hit my face I wake up. Always at the same point.

I look at the plane ticket in my hand and I smile. I really truly smile.

–

DOCTOR: The patient is deteriorating, his grip on
reality is starting to loosen.

I have been dabbling with the idea of
institutionalising him. Sending him to the cuckoo's
nest, cuckoo, cuckoo…

Fading in and out of lucidity.

I ordered a couch… Not the one I wanted.

The thing that is confusing is that I can't figure
out if I am real or a figment of his fevered
imagination…

I call myself a Dr, I have 'Dr' written on my jacket
and on a small plastic sign that sits on my desk but
for the life of me I don't feel like I know anything
about medicine. I don't remember going to
medical school, I don't really remember anything.
Look, this desk, this stuff, none of it's real, look
it's plastic, this notepad that I've been writing in
all this time, it doesn't even have notes in, just
squiggly lines.

Note to self – Ask Janet if I am real.

Note to self – Ask Janet if she is real.

He presses a buzzer on his desk.

DCOTOR: Janet!?

JANET: *(Over Intercom.)* Yes.

DCOTOR: Are you real?

She doesn't answer.

DOCTOR: Janet? JANET! Oh for God's sake.
Dennis if you can hear me, if you can hear this
snap out of it. Pull yourself together!

—

DENNIS is back in his plane seat.

DENNIS: *(V.O.)* The buzzing... It was quiet at first; I could barely hear it over the roar of the engine. I thought it was in my head, a sign of my panic, or my discomfort with the flight. Perhaps my ears, the pressure. I hold my nose, close my eyes and blow as hard as I can. I feel my ears pop as the pressure is released but it is still there.

Buzz buzz buzz.

DENNIS: No no no... Come on...no
How is this even possible, on a plane? Where did it...? How could it...?

Buzz buzz buzz.

DENNIS: *(V.O.)* I feel a sharp, stabbing pain in my stomach.

DENNIS: No, please...

Buzz buzz buzz.

DENNIS: *(V.O.)* I close my eyes tightly wishing with every atom in my being that I could be somewhere else. Willing my body to disintegrate, particle by particle and to float away somewhere else. But my flesh remains stubbornly solid.

Buzz buzz buzz.

DENNIS: *(V.O.)* I clutch the arm rests.

Grinding my teeth into powder.
My breath starts to quicken.

Buzz buzz buzz.

DENNIS: *(V.O.)* I'm trapped. Trapped, there is nothing I can do, trapped with my tormentor.

Buzz buzz buzz.

DENNIS V.O. (In woman's voice.)
Are you ok honey?
Says the blimp beside me, clearly concerned.
I bark a kind of response but keep my eyes firmly closed.

Buzz buzz buzz.

DENNIS: No please…

Buzz buzz buzz.

DENNIS: Help me…
Buzz buzz bu…

DENNIS: *(V.O.)* Then suddenly it stops. Silence…the calm.

WOMAN: *Dear? Would you like me to get someone…?*

DENNIS: *(V.O.)* I release my jaw, and open my eyes, turning to look at her and then I see it.
Sitting there, perched on the top of her immaculately groomed thatch of hair, staring at me.
I gasp, glaring at it.

She looks back at me, her eyes starting to widen with alarm.

WOMAN: *...Are you ok?*

DENNIS: *(V.O.)* Its legs twitch slightly. This is it, kill or be killed.

WOMAN: *Dear...?*

DENNIS: *(V.O.)* Without taking my eyes off of it, I steel myself, reaching forward, slowly I take the in-flight magazine and start rolling it up, tightly.
The blimp watches me nervously.
I grip it firmly, my breath is erratic, sweat pours down my forehead, my hands are shaking.

WOMAN: *Dear...?*

DENNIS: *(V.O.)* I have no choice...

Beat.

DENNIS: *(Addressing the audience.)* Flies have this ability...an instinct, it's like a defence mechanism, that when something comes at them, to swat them they see it and within 200 milliseconds the fly calculates the location of the threat and positions its legs for a jump in the safest direction. Avoiding the oncoming danger.
...humans don't have this ability.

We see a brief glimpse of DENNIS' attack on the woman.

–

PILOT ANNOUNCMENT: Ladies and gentlemen, this is your pilot speaking, I am very sorry to report that we shall be performing a premature landing for today's flight to Antarctica, this is due to someone attacking another passenger with their complimentary copy of Whizz magazine which can be found in your seat backs.

I can confirm the victim is ok though somewhat shaken and the passenger in question has been suitably restrained by a member of our cabin crew. I'm extremely sorry for the disruption this will cause to your journey; the passenger in question is called Dennis and is sitting in seat 62A so please feel free to direct all your frustration and anger towards him for the remaining duration of the flight.

To be honest it's a real shame Dennis, a real shame. I'm not even angry. I'm disappointed. You've let your fellow passengers down and more importantly, you've let yourself down. You were doing so well. You were so close – Just a few hours away from your new life, your freedom and you throw it all away. Silly. Silly silly silly.

I want you to sit there and think about what you did.

Boo Dennis, boo to you. Booo.

Everybody please Boooooooo. Not only has he spoilt it for himself but he's spoilt it for the rest of us, thanks a lot buddy...you've let us all down...literally.

Booo.

–

DENNIS: I return home to my empty flat.

Just stains where 'things' used to be. My stuff has gone, sold to strangers to pay for my plane ticket, it's starting a new life and I am left behind.

I think of my sofa wandering around its new home, making new friends, starting fresh, no ties, no expectations, becoming the sofa it always wanted to be, the sofa it always knew it could be if only it weren't held back by circumstance.

Maybe it won't even be a sofa anymore; maybe it'll choose to be a lamp or a sink.

I sit and stare at the blank walls, bubbling with jealousy towards my absent sofa.

I look at the windows that won't open.

I breathe the stale air.

And I sink to a new low.

–

FLY: I watch you… All the time, I'm there, seeing what you're doing. The little buzzing in your head. That's me. In the kitchen, in the bathroom.

When you sleep I land on your face, I crawl into your mouth and up your nose. I creep around your hair. My faecal feet padding around your skin whilst you dream about me, whilst you have nightmares about me.

And you don't even realise that whilst you are inside the cavern of that nightmare, outside, I am there, with you.

I crawl down your throat, I get caught in your windpipe.

When you are hot and sweaty I will get all up in your fucking face.

I will crawl in your ear. I will creep slowly into your brain. I will settle behind your eyeball. I will flap my tiny little wings as hard as I can. I will beat those little fuckers as fast as I can – Beat them till they snap. Buzz Buzz Buzz.

So hard, so fast behind your eyeballs, Buzz Buzz, like an itch you can't scratch, Buzz Buzz Buzz, right in the centre of your skull and I will buzz so hard until I die from sheer exhaustion.

And then my corpse will rot and decay and decompose inside your face.

Until my stinking rotting carcass starts to attract the attention of more and more tiny flies – Who will come for you and find you, and crawl into your nose and ears and eyes, Buzz Buzz Buzz – all desperate to feast on my rotting cadaver.

They will vomit and defecate inside your head. They will lay their eggs, which will grow into larvae and maggots who'll crawl around inside your skull. Eating your brain from the inside out, feasting on your mind until there's nothing of it left.

Then they will shit it all out and die and the whole thing will start all over again.

Over and over and over, for all eternity.

And you know why all of this happens. Because I don't like you.

–

DENNIS speaks, but something seems to have changed in him.

DENNIS: I have been thinking a lot about what the
    Doctor has said, about confronting and defeating

my fear. About the best way forward, my best
chance of doing this.

And I have decided to become a spider…

Initially I feared that this decision would prove
rather redundant. I mean, surely there is more to
being a spider than just *deciding* to be one. There
are physiological differences. Would I just remain
me simply sitting in my room saying 'I'm a spider'
over and over?

However, I was surprised how quickly things
started to change once the decision was made.
Perhaps I had underestimated the power of my
own convictions but within days thick coarse black
hairs started to appear on my body. At first they
hurt as they pierced through the surface of my
skin but soon I don't notice, I become numb to it,
almost finding the pain comforting. In less than a
week my arms are virtually covered in them.

FLY: The old lady, that was me.

DENNIS: I start to experience pain in my gums. As I
sleep my mouth fills with teeth, my useless blunt
cudmunching molars are slowly being pushed out.
They are being replaced by new, sharp venomous
fangs.

I spit out the mouthfuls of useless calcium lumps
and run my tongue over the points.

FLY: The scientist, that was me.

DENNIS: I start to lose differentiation between my
limbs, arms seem to become legs. It's disorientating
at first but soon I start to acclimatise.

FLY: The Babies.

DENNIS: My vision starts to change – Naturally. It's like I can feel my eyeballs separating. Multiplying, like cells.

FLY: The Egyptians.

DENNIS: Lumps begin to appear at my ribs – hard, bony, stumps. I think these are my new legs.

FLY: The Fly that will buzz when you die.

DENNIS: I remove the tape from the plug sockets and the taps. I watch closely as I peel it off, expecting a sudden flood, pouring through but it doesn't happen.
Nothing happens.

FLY: Because I don't like you.

DENNIS: I watch these entry points for a number of hours and realise, rather than fear, what I feel is anticipation. I'm excited, almost like I want them to appear.

FLY: I don't like you.

DENNIS: I'm hungry.

DENNIS turns into a spider.

FLY: Dennis…? Dennis…? DENNIS?

–

DOCTOR's surgery – everything seems more 'real' than it has previously.

DOCTOR: Dennis, how are you?

DENNIS: Ok.

DOCTOR: Have you been well?

DENNIS doesn't answer.

DOCTOR: Have you thought about what we discussed at the last session? Some of the options available? The cognitive therapy? Hypnotherapy?

DENNIS: I don't like the idea of being hypnotised.

DOCTOR: Dennis I'm going to have to write a report, about your condition…for the court. They want to know whether to press charges, whether you pose a threat. It would help your cause if you at least appeared to be trying to resolve the problem.

DENNIS: I'm here.

DOCTOR: This is true. And do you think it's helping? Talking about it?

DENNIS: I don't know.

DOCTOR: Well do you feel any different?

DENNIS: Yes.

DOCTOR: Well that's a good start. Look, I deal with people every day who are scared of something, heights, crocodiles, balloons. It's very natural and it's very easy to resolve it was me.

DENNIS looks at the DOCTOR confused.

DENNIS: What was you?

DOCTOR: Excuse me?

DENNIS: You said it was you.

DOCTOR: I said what was me?

DENNIS: I don't know, that's what you said.

DOCTOR: Ok, well I guess what I was saying is that I have helped lots of people just like you to overcome these… crippling fears, but that I need you to work with me and that it was me on the plane.

DENNIS: What?

DOCTOR: On the plane that was me.

DENNIS: What are you talking about?

DOCTOR: …I'm saying I want to help you Dennis.

DENNIS stares at him, the DOCTOR is confused.

DENNIS: You were on the plane…?

DOCTOR: The plane? Do you want to talk about what happened on the plane?

DENNIS: No.

DOCTOR: Ok Dennis look let's focus a little bit.

He opens his drawer and pulls out a plate of biscuits, offering them to DENNIS.

DOCTOR: Biscuit?

DENNIS: No thank you.

DOCTOR: Do you mind if I?

DENNIS: No of course.

DOCTOR: Great.

> *The DOCTOR disappears behind his desk and we hear a horrible sound of eating and vomiting. DENNIS is very disturbed. After a moment the DOCTOR reappears wiping his mouth.*

DOCTOR: That's better now where were we?

DENNIS: What are you doing?

DOCTOR: Excuse me?

DENNIS: Who are you?

DOCTOR: Dennis it's Dr Rickman, you've been seeing me for the last six weeks. Are you feeling alright?

DENNIS: What do you want from me?

DOCTOR: I just want to help you and crawl down your throat.

> *DENNIS stands alarmed.*

DOCTOR: Ok Dennis just calm down.

DENNIS: Stay away from me!

DOCTOR: Jesus you fucking baby!

DENNIS: What?

DOCTOR: There was an old woman who swallowed a fly, I don't know why she swallowed a fly, perhaps she'll die.

DENNIS stares at the DOCTOR, who then returns to normal.

DOCTOR: Dennis, please just sit down, you're getting upset. Dennis…

DENNIS stares at him, scared.

DOCTOR: It's ok, this is a safe place, it's just me, I'm here to help you.

DENNIS calms down and sits.

DOCTOR: We have to find a way through this. You can't let this beat you. You must confront it, beat it, otherwise your life will always be dictated by this fear. You have to take ownership of it, find a way through it. You have to defeat it or it will defeat you.

He puts his hand on DENNIS' shoulder. DENNIS nods. After a beat we hear the sound of buzzing, the DOCTOR returns to his chair.

He starts to whistle 'There was an old woman who swallowed a fly.'

DENNIS looks up. The DOCTOR continues to whistle the tune.

DENNIS spots a fly buzzing around his head. He follows its path.

Suddenly out of nowhere DENNIS reaches his two hands into the air lighting-quick, slapping them together and catching the fly.

The DOCTOR looks up, startled. DENNIS slowly looks at the DOCTOR.

Blackout.

We hear the sound effects of a struggle accompanied by remnants of the happy 'Winter Wonderland' music from the top of the show.

Possibly in the dark we can just make out the DOCTOR being wrapped up, as if in a web.

The End.

OTHER OLIVER LANSLEY TITLES

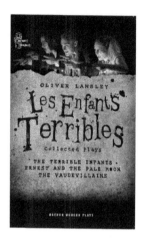

Les Enfants Terribles: Collected Plays
THE TERRIBLE INFANTS
ERNEST AND THE PALE MOON
THE VAUDEVILLAINS

£12.99 / 9781849431637

Les Enfants Terribles: Collected Plays presents a thematic trilogy of plays from one of Britain's most innovative theatre companies. As a document of the company's progress over its ten-year history, the collection also features production photos, design sketches and introductions to each play. *The Terrible Infants* (2007) blends puppetry, live music, performance and storytelling to present a series of twisted tales for children and adults. Inspired by the likes of Edgar Allan Poe and Alfred Hitchcock. *Ernest and the Pale Moon* (2009) is a noir horror based upon a tale of murderous envy. *The Vaudevillains* (2010) is a dark miniature musical whodunnit…when the owner of The Empire music hall is murdered, everyone's a suspect….

'A talented company with a very sure sense of its own distinctive storytelling style.' – *Guardian*

'Oliver Lansley of Les Enfants Terribles has found that winning formula of talent, charm and absolute irreverence' – *The Stage*

THE INFANT

by oliver lansley

OBERON MODERN PLAYS

The Infant
£9.99 / 9781849432283

Are we paranoid? Or are they really out to get us?

They have a picture, a picture that could spell the destruction of civilised society, a plan so devastating it would change the world as we know it. They must put a stop to it. They have a suspect, tied to a chair, a hood covering his face. The only problem is the suspect claims the picture was drawn by his four-year-old son. They have the suspect's wife, but she claims her son couldn't have made the picture. Who's telling the truth? What is the truth? And does the truth really matter any more?

'The Infant is a highly assured, absurdist piece with many resonances for today's climate of fear, suspicion and arbitrary justice... This clever premise develops through interrogations, violence and circular logic into a penetrating look at police paranoia and state-led authoritarianism. Lansley shows himself a gifted playwright'
– The Stage

WWW.OBERONBOOKS.COM

 Follow us on www.twitter.com/@oberonbooks
& www.facebook.com/oberonbook